Biblical
ALLEGORIES
Uncovering the Depths
of God's Word

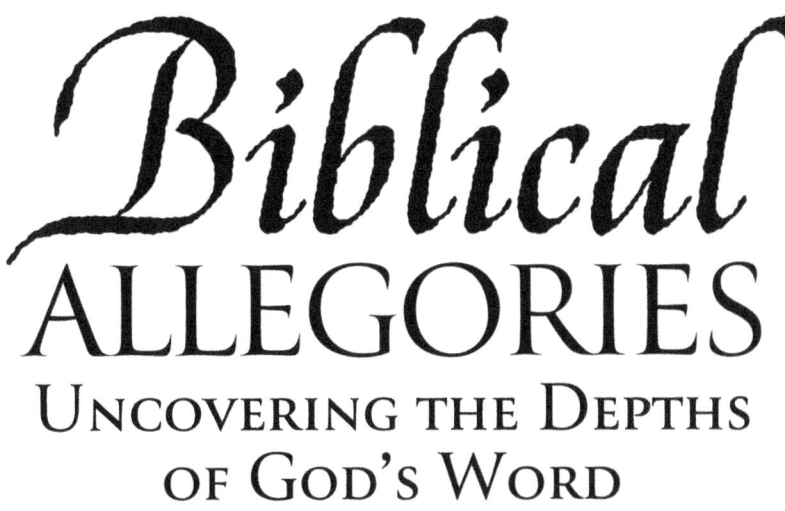

Biblical ALLEGORIES

UNCOVERING THE DEPTHS OF GOD'S WORD

EDWARD THAL

AUTHOR OF *REDISCOVERING THE PRESENCE OF GOD*

Other books by Edward Thal

The Victorious Christian Life
Rediscovering the Presence of God
Transcendent Christ
Glory in the Church
Leadership Lessons from the Life of Joshua
This One Thing
The Broken Altar

For Kyle Fannin
My pastor and dear friend

CONTENTS

INTRODUCTION

THE GREAT PROPHET JEREMIAH DECLARED: *Thy words were found, and I did eat them; and thy word was unto me the joy and rejoicing of my heart. (Jeremiah 15:16)*

Just as the food we eat becomes a part of us, providing daily nourishment, so is the Word of God. The Bible is as life-giving yet as basic and uncomplicated as bread. It is written not for us to debate, but to digest; it is food for the soul, not for gourmets but for the hungry. It is a storybook that unfolds a simple message from beginning to end: We are sinners; God has provided a Savior.

To aid our understanding and make the teaching accessible even to children, much of the story is told in the form of parables and allegories, word pictures whose messages are easily grasped. Historical events in the Old Testament turn out to illustrate deep spiritual truths when viewed from the perspective of the New Testament, or from our personal experience.

An allegory is defined as the representation of ideas or principles by characters, figures, or events in narrative or dramatic form. More simply put, allegories are "word pictures." They appear throughout Scripture as aids to understanding or remembering spiritual truths. Many details in an allegory are merely part of the story, not themselves principles to be adopted. For example, a blind person would not assume from the story in John 9 that the key to receiving physical sight is to sit at a roadside with a begging bowl—the lesson is the outcome of a blind beggar's encounter with Jesus. The full impact of the story is felt when we come to understand that before our salvation we are the blind beggar!

The Apostle Paul carefully explains an allegory when he unpacks references to the first two sons of Abraham and likens them to the Old Covenant and New Covenant, to the bondwoman (Hagar) and the freewoman (Sarah), to Mount Sinai and Mount Zion, to flesh and spirit, to earthly Jerusalem and heavenly New Jerusalem (see Galatians 4:21-5:1). In Romans 15:4 and I Corinthians 10:1-6,11 he declares that stories about Old Testament events are examples and types written for our instruction.

In the next few pages, we will seek to bring some key allegories to life, exploring the depth, the consistency, and the power of God's Word that teaches us everything we need to know about our Origin, Purpose, Morality and Destiny.

CHAPTER ONE

LEPROSY, BLINDNESS AND THE LAMB

AN OUTWARD, VISIBLE SIGN OF an inward sickness, leprosy was a disease regarded by the ancient Hebrews as a direct punishment from God for a great transgression.

The disease eats inwards to the bones and outwards on the flesh. Like spiritual corruption it spreads gradually, eventually disfiguring the whole body just as sin defiles and corrupts our inner nature. Lepers were segregated from society and were not allowed to enter the Temple, just as sinners are separated from the presence of God.

And the leper in whom the plague is,
his clothes shall be rent, and his head bare,
and he shall put a covering on his upper lip,
and shall cry, "Unclean, unclean!"
All the days wherein the plague shall be in him

1

shall he be defiled, he is unclean, He shall dwell alone,
without the camp shall his habitation be. (Lev. 13:45-46)

God's children (you and me, for example), are adept at excusing or even denying our own sins. At the very least, we downplay the serious nature of sin. Back in Old Testament days it was impossible to downplay leprosy's presence and destructiveness, as graphically illustrated by the Levitical Law and regulations for the identification and treatment of the sickness (see Leviticus chapters 13 and 14.) Central to the cure was a sacrificial lamb whose blood would make atonement for the sickness. When a priest confirmed that a cure was indeed evident, a bird was killed, and its blood was mixed with water. Then a second bird was immersed in the blood and water before being released to fly away, just as our sins "fly away" when washed in the blood of our Savior.

A dramatic illustration of the analogy between sin and leprosy is provided in Numbers 12, where Miriam opposes Moses and becomes leprous. A story about the humility required to receive healing from God is told in 2 Kings chapter 5 where we learn of a great Syrian general who seeks deliverance for his affliction from the Prophet Elisha. The key passage appears in chapter 5:9-14.

The New Testament presents the fulfillment of Old Testament prophecy and the Law as Jesus constantly heals lepers, often in a way that nobody else would dare to do: He reached out and touched them (Matthew 8:2-3).

Blindness is mentioned 150 times in the Bible and is symbolic of the inability to perceive spiritual truth as demonstrated in Corinthians and Ephesians:

But if our gospel is hid it is hid to them that are lost:
in whom the god of this world hath blinded the minds
of them which believe not, lest the light of the glorious gospel of Christ,
who is the image of God, should shine unto them (2 Cor. 4:3-4).
Walk not as other Gentiles walk, in the vanity of their mind,
having the understanding darkened, being alienated
from the life of God through the ignorance that is in them,
because of the blindness of their heart. (Ephesians 4:17-18).

The saddest illustration of spiritual blindness and impotence is found in the story of Samson, a man greatly blessed by God whose spiritual immaturity and carnality caused him to lose his eyes and sink to the level of a donkey, grinding a mill, blindly going in circles, getting nowhere. (Judges 16:18-21).

By contrast, the most dramatic story of sight being restored appears in the story of the conversion of Saul, found in Acts 9:3-9 and 17-18. Healing blindness was a major part of Christ's earthly ministry. The story of the man born blind in John 9 provides a complete testimony of the impact of personal soul winning and the restoration of spiritual sight.

Scripture's most powerful pictorial allegory appears in constant references throughout both the Old Testament and New Testament to the sacrificial death of a lamb as a remedy for sin. The innocence of lambs, their vulnerability, and their pure white wool points to the character of a perfect Savior who paid a debt He did not owe for a price mankind could never pay.

Illustrations and prophetic references abound in accounts like Abraham sacrificing Isaac (Genesis 22:1-18), Israel sacrificing lambs in Egypt to escape the death angel (Exodus 12:1-28), the Feast of Passover (Exodus 12:14), and worship that included sacrifices in the Tabernacle and Temple.

The great prophet Isaiah spoke of the fulfillment of the Feast of Passover (53:4-7). 1,500 years after the Exodus, and 600 years after Isaiah, the true Lamb and His purpose was identified, as recorded in John 1:29. Then the Lamb was sacrificed, at the appointed time (Luke 22:1-7).

Finally, we see the Lamb triumphant in the Revelation. In this prophetic book about the end times there are 22 references to the Lamb. Revelation 5:1-14 shows the Lamb as Sacrifice and King and God. Revelation 12:11 reminds us that we overcome the world, the flesh, and the devil "by the blood of the Lamb," and by our testimony. At the end of the prophecy, we are told that everything culminates in the Lamb: Revelation 21: 9-10, 22-27; 22:1-3.

These accounts in Revelation help us to appreciate the magnificence of our Savior and His extraordinary love for us that caused Him to stoop so low to bring us salvation. In the next chapter we will explore just how low we do fall from God's grace as we survey the life of Jacob and his bumpy road from cheat and deceiver to God's Prince.

CHAPTER TWO

LESSONS FROM THE LIFE OF JACOB

THE THREE FATHERS OF THE Hebrew faith are mentioned together numerous times in Scripture for good reason – not only to identify the God of the Hebrews but also to characterize God's people. (See Exodus 3:13-15). Allegorical references abound.

In Abraham, God supports the faithful. In Isaac, He keeps His promises. In Jacob, He furthers His purpose. Abraham is saved through his faith in God that later results in the miraculous "spiritual" birth of Isaac, whose name means laughter, reminding us that salvation brings joy (Isaiah 2:3).

Jacob's life illustrates the war between our two natures – flesh and spirit – that follows our spiritual birth. His twin brother Esau, born first, is earthy, unspiritual, and sells his inheritance as the eldest son for things that please him. Jacob, who takes hold of the birthright, is always in conflict—with himself, with his brother, with his father, with his father-in-law, with his own

5

sons, and always finds a way to prevail, until he wrestles with God. The story is told from Genesis 25:19 to the end of chapter 32, where we see Jacob physically crippled but spiritually whole.

The allegorical contrast between Esau and Jacob, flesh and spirit, is vividly highlighted by Paul's explanation to the Corinthians of the differences between Adam, the first man, and Jesus, identified as the last Adam, whose death on the cross marked not only death to our old nature but the end of God's relationship with fallen humanity. Christ's resurrection established Him as the second man, the progenitor of a new race of humans who would enjoy an eternal relationship with God (Ephesians 2:1).

Paul begins by explaining the nature of the resurrection body (1 Corinthians 15:35-44) before contrasting the difference between a living soul and a life-giving spirit (verses 45-47). Adam was the first-born of the human race who (long before Esau) traded his divine inheritance for the forbidden fruit (personal fulfillment) and was separated from God. When Jesus died on the Cross He represented the last of the earthly Adamic race, but He did not stay locked in the grave. He rose from the dead as the "second Man", founder of a new, spiritual race descended, not from earth, but from heaven. We are born again into that new humanity when Christ's resurrection life becomes ours at salvation. This explains Paul chiding the sinful Christians at Corinth for behaving like mere men, descendants of the first Adam (1 Corinthians 3:3).

Against this background, the story of Jacob the supplanter (one who takes the place of someone who was there first) is fascinating in its Scriptural detail. Genesis 25:21-34 sets the stage for the character of Jacob and provides a dramatic backdrop for his later transformation into someone very different. Three additional passages of Scripture sum up his life.

At his beginning: *Is not he rightly named Jacob? For he hath supplanted me these two times: he took away my birthright, and behold, now he hath taken away my blessing. (Genesis 27:36)*

At his end: *By faith Jacob, when he was dying, blessed both the sons of Joseph; and worshipped, leaning upon the top of his staff. (Hebrews 11:21)*

His motivation in between is vividly summarized by the Apostle Paul in reference to his own determined reaching for a spiritual life so different from the successes and failures of his earthly life:

This one thing I do, forgetting those things which are behind, and reaching forth unto the things which are before, I press towards the mark for the prize of the high calling of God in Christ Jesus. (Philippians 3:13-14)

The details of Jacob's progress through life – from supplanter to saint – takes on special significance when we relate it to our personal journey. He did not travel in miles as far as his grandfather Abraham; but he did travel a very great distance in his spiritual growth. The name given to him by his parents at birth described him very well: *Jacob* means supplanter (in colloquial terms, "claim jumper"); the name later given to him by the Angel of the Lord marked the outcome of his striving and eventual spiritual transformation: *Israel*, Prince of God (Genesis 32:28).

Clearly, Jacob's character and life is a rich allegory about you and me.

His life is filled with deception:
- He deceives his father (with the death of a lamb to supplant Esau: Genesis 25:29)
- He is deceived by his father-in-law (the deceiver deceived: Genesis 29:16-25)
- His sons deceive the family of Hamor (Genesis 34)
- He is deceived by his sons (who sell Joseph into slavery and sprinkle the blood of a lamb on his coat to fake his death: Gen. 37:31-35)

His life is full of fights and divisions
- Two brothers fight - Esau and Jacob (even before birth!)
- Two sisters fight - Leah and Rachel (Genesis 30:1-21)
- Laban and Jacob fight (Genesis 31)
- Jacob fights with God (Genesis 32)

At last Jacob meets his match, and is crippled (Genesis 32:24-31)

Only then does he become God's Prince (Israel). Humbled, he learns to be thoughtful, sensitive, and loving (Genesis 33:12-14)

Jacob, like the Apostle Paul, was constantly pushing and striving towards a goal that he barely perceived. But in a life full of conflict Jacob's ultimate battle was with God. It left him broken yet transformed. He was forced to confess who he was and be crippled before he could be renamed the Prince of God. The Apostle Paul learned the same lesson.

He [God] said unto me, My grace is sufficient for thee,
for my strength is made perfect in weakness.
Most gladly therefore will I rather glory in my infirmities,
that the power of Christ may rest upon me. (2 Cor. 12:9)

When Jacob was broken by God he was fundamentally changed. The striver, the supplanter, the fighter became a careful man, still with faults, but more considerate, and worshipful, as we saw in Gen. 33:12-14. In the New Testament memorial to Old Testament heroes, Jacob receives the ultimate accolade when he is remembered not as a supplanter, or a deceiver, or a fighter with God and man, but as a worshipper!

By faith Jacob, when he was a dying, blessed both the sons of Joseph
and worshipped, leaning upon the top of his staff. (Hebrews 11:21)

SPIRITUAL LESSONS FROM THE LIFE OF JACOB

Until we get hold of God, and God gets hold of us, nothing else in this life matters. Jacob's story clearly illustrates that God is more interested in our passion for him than in our performance, good or bad. Jacob was not a very nice person. He was deceitful and greedy and selfish. But he would not let go of God, and God transformed him!

Note that Jesus condemned the Laodiceans, not for being sinful but for being lukewarm (Revelation 3:14-20). This is not an encouragement to sin, but to be passionate in our relationship with God.

So let us emulate Jacob, and not Esau. Resolve not to be a part-time Christian, a convenience Christian, a once-a-week Christian – but turn to the Lord, and ask Him to deal with your cold heart, and stir up your spirit, and touch you as He touched Jacob, and turn you from a sinner into a saint!

From the story of Moses leading the Israelites out of slavery in Egypt to the Promised Land we learn that such transformation is neither easy nor quick. What should have been a journey of weeks in terms of the physical distance covered took 40 years because of the rebelliousness and sinfulness of God's people. Their old attitudes and ways had to endure a long and winding trail before a surviving remnant could begin to appreciate and understand their relationship with God. When a new generation at last stood ready to enter the land flowing with milk and honey, Moses urged them to be single-minded and obedient in their walk with God. (Note that the Promised Land is not a picture of heaven, but of the victorious, Christ-centered life we are called to experience here on earth.)

I call heaven and earth to record this day against you,
that I have set before you life and death,

blessing and cursing: therefore choose life...

that thou mayest love the Lord thy God,

and that thou mayest obey his voice,

and that thou mayest cleave to him, for he is thy life,

and the length of thy days,

that thou mayest dwell in the land which the Lord sware

unto thy fathers, to Abraham, to Isaac, and to Jacob...

(Deuteronomy 30:19-20)

CHAPTER THREE

AMALEK!

ALLEGORIES ASSOCIATED WITH THE CONFLICT between our old nature ("flesh") and our new nature in Christ ("spirit"), are among the most powerful and consistent in Scripture because the issue is vital to every Christian.

Before the struggles of Jacob and his conflict with Esau, discussed in the previous chapter, there was the rivalry between Cain and Abel (Genesis 4:1-8), and Ishmael and Isaac (Genesis 21:5-10). There was conflict in the wilderness between the many who complained and the few who conquered (Deuteronomy 1:27-36). The New Testament introduces the so-called Prodigal Son and his older brother (Luke 15:25-30), and in the Apostle John we see a former "Son of Thunder" (Mark 3:17, probably a reference to calling fire from heaven on the Samaritans, recorded in Luke 9:54), transformed into the Apostle associated most with God's message of Love.

The Apostle Paul has much to say on the subject of flesh and spirit. He ties the sons of Abraham, Ishmael and Isaac, to the Old Covenant and New Covenant, to the bondwoman (Hagar) and the freewoman (Sarah), to Mount Sinai and Mount Zion, to earthly Jerusalem and heavenly New Jerusalem (Galatians 4:21-5:1). In his letter to the Romans, he declares:

I know that in me (that is, in my flesh), dwelleth no good thing
They that are after the flesh do mind the things of the flesh,
but they that are after the Spirit the things of the Spirit.
For to be carnally minded is death; but to be spiritually minded is life
and peace. Because the carnal mind is enmity against God: for it is
not subject to the law of God, neither indeed can be. So then they that
are in the flesh cannot please God. If ye live after the flesh ye shall die:
but if ye through the Spirit do mortify the deeds of the body,
ye shall live. (Romans 7:18; 8:5-8, 13
There is therefore now no condemnation to them which are in Christ Jesus,
who walk not after the flesh but after the Spirit (Romans 8:1)

The apostle makes it clear that the old nature is our sinful human nature that was part of us at birth. We are not born perfect! (For a vivid demonstration of the old nature, place two toddlers in a room with only one toy!) Discipline does not eradicate the old nature, just harnesses it like a bridle in the mouth of a horse. Our new nature, on the other hand, is received when we are born again. It is the Resurrection Life of Jesus Christ in us and is strengthened as we voluntarily submit to Him.

In this chapter we will go back to the Old Testament to trace the strange and sinister appearance and reappearance of Amalek, whose story begins in Genesis. By the time we read of a final encounter between Amalek and Esther 1,500 years later we may understand that a victorious Christian life is impossible if we neither know nor care about a war to the death with our old, corrupt nature that begins at salvation and does not end until our triumphant entry into heaven.

If you have read the previous chapter you will not be surprised to learn that Amalek is the grandson of Esau, who sold his birthright for immediate carnal gratification. (Genesis 25:31-32; with 36:12). We next meet Amalek immediately after Israel's escape from Egypt. For more rich allegory, note that Israel was saved in Egypt from the Death Angel by the blood of a lamb (Exodus 12), departed Egypt by "baptism" in the Red Sea (Exodus 14), received life-giving water from a Rock (later identified with Christ, I Corinthians 10:4) and then suffered attack by Amalek (Exodus 17:8-16), who arrived on the scene without introduction and without warning.

Then came Amalek and fought with Israel in Rephidim (17:8).

"Rephidim" is a Hebrew word that indicates a place of rest. As the battle progresses we note that prayer defeats Amalek (Exodus 17:11), but the enemy prevails when Israel's spiritual leader, Moses, grows weary. The powerful allegorical picture is completed as Aaron and Hur stand on either side of Moses and hold up his hands until Amalek is driven from the field of battle. The Lord announces his intention to obliterate all memory of this determined adversary, instructing Moses to build a memorial altar named "The Lord is My Banner" (Jehovah-nissi).

Because the Lord hath sworn that the Lord will have war with Amalek from generation to generation (Exodus 17:16).

This reference underlines the obvious fact that our enemy is also God's enemy! We can't compromise with our old nature: it cannot be tamed, it cannot be improved, it must not be indulged, it must die! Jesus declares to His disciples that they must take up their cross—an instrument of death—if they intend to follow Him (Matthew 16:24). The single rule in our war against the flesh is to obey God. If we indulge our flesh—our unspiritual, carnal nature—it will kill us (perhaps literally, certainly spiritually). Have no mercy on Amalek!

Remember what Amalek did unto thee by the way, when ye were come forth out of Egypt,
how he met then by the way, and smote the hindmost of thee,
even all that were feeble behind thee, when thou wast faint and weary,
and he feared not God.
Therefore, it shall be when the Lord thy God hath given thee rest
from all thine enemies round about, in the land which the Lord thy God giveth thee
for an inheritance to possess it, that thou shalt blot out the remembrance of Amalek
from under heaven, thou shalt not forget it. (Deuteronomy 25:17-19).

Scripture provides a powerful warning through the life of Israel's first king of the consequences if we fail to obey God.

King Saul indulged Amalek, (1 Samuel 15:1-3, 7-9, 16-23), and Amalek killed him: (2 Samuel 1:1-10, especially verse 8). Amalek remained a constant threat to Israel, always seeking their destruction, even years later when they were captive in a foreign land (Esther 3:1; 8-10; 8:3-5). Note that Haman, the villain in this story, was descended from the royal line of Amalek, whose kings carried the title of Agag.

Our duty is clear: *Make not provision for the flesh, to fulfill the lusts thereof (Romans 13:14).*

Instead, plunge completely into God's Will, God's Way, and experience God's Wonderful Life, as we are encouraged to do in Ezekiel 47:1-5.

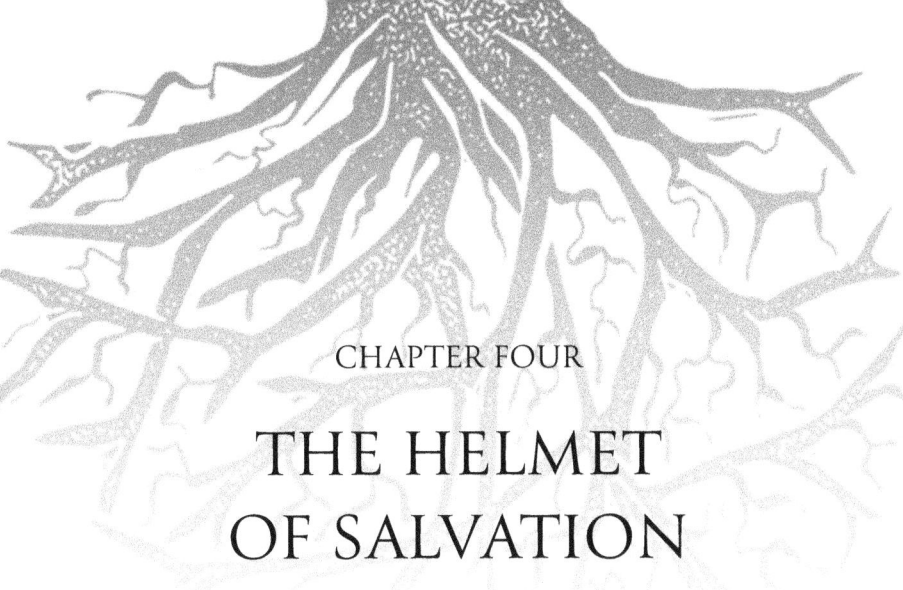

CHAPTER FOUR

THE HELMET
OF SALVATION

WE BEGAN OUR EXPLORATION OF Biblical Allegories by noting that all humans are born suffering from "leprosy" and "blindness" – two allegorical conditions in Scripture that depict our corrupt inner nature and inability to know Truth – inherited as a result of the downfall of Adam and Eve and their banishment from the presence of God. The only cure is the atonement offered by the sacrificial Lamb of God.

Yet, glorious as it is, God's incarnation, perfect life and voluntary death as a criminal in our place, initially delivers us only from the penalty for our sinful condition. This was the powerful work of Calvary to which we can add nothing, but it is left to us to discover the power of the Resurrection. We must continue to work out our salvation with God's help. It is His work in us that produces the desire and the effort to obey Him (Philippians

17

2:12-13); our work is to continue the struggle to overcome a sin nature that has been crippled but not destroyed.

The struggle lasts a lifetime and is essential to build our spiritual strength and Christian character. If this phase of our Christian experience is as instant and complete as our deliverance from the penalty for sin, we would learn nothing about the extent of our weakness and depravity, and little about the power of God as it applies to our condition. And having learned little we would be able to teach little to those who come after us. Jacob's life experiences still teach us today, just as Amalek's story reminds us that we must be unrelenting in our war against our old nature.

In the Old Testament, warfare is a notable aspect of the experience of God's people from the moment they leave Egypt, and it does not stop when they enter the Promised Land of Milk and Honey. In fact, the war intensifies in the Promised Land – there are a lot more enemies, and some of them are giants! (See Numbers 13:26-33). This should come as no surprise to us if we decipher God's purpose from His rebuke to the errant King Saul (1 Samuel 15:17-19): we are not delivered from lives of sin and futility so that we can pursue our personal aims and opinions or satisfy our own desires. We are saved to serve God alone, and the way God keeps us close to Him is to confront us with challenges that we cannot overcome without His help. If we stick close to God and draw on His strength, victory is assured, and is often surprisingly easy; if we disobey, our sins and the problems they bring will be a constant source of discouragement and defeat.

Reading the Books of Joshua and Judges with these thoughts in mind will reveal their history as a series of rich allegorical lessons to guide us in our walk with God. The many compromises recorded in Judges 1:19-21;27-33 would later cause the downfall of Israel. A summary of the consequences in Judges 2:1-4 is followed by God's angry response to persistent disobedience (Judges 10:10-14). Also note the folly of making promises to God to secure His deliverance from the consequences of our disobedience. A better response is repentance and faith! (Judges 11:30-35).

To sum up, spiritual warfare is an inescapable feature of the Christian life. Our salvation is much more than an escape from punishment and a ticket to heaven; it is an invasion by our Creator of the entire human being! It sparks a radical transformation where "all things are become new" (2 Corinthians 5:17) and all the "old things" become our enemies. We trace our new ancestry to a new Father, through a new birth that makes us citizens of a new kingdom:

Except a man be born again, he cannot see the
Kingdom of God (John 3:3)

[God] hath delivered us from the power of darkness,
And hath translated us into the kingdom of His dear Son
(Colossians 1:13)

Our new birth makes us sing a new song (Ps. 40:1-3), and adds much more:

A new heart also will I give you,
and a new spirit will I put within you,
and I will take away the stony heart out of your flesh
and I will give you a heart of flesh.
And I will put my spirit within you,
and cause you to walk in my statutes,
and ye shall keep my judgments and do them.
And ye shall dwell in the land that I gave to your fathers, and ye shall
*   be my people, and I will be your God.*
(Ezekiel 36:26-28)

If you're wondering what all of this has to do with wearing a helmet, we have arrived at the answer: the war we face is a spiritual one, salvation means being drafted as a soldier in this war to the death, and the battleground is our mind. The change of "heart" at the time of salvation is a change to our inner core. That change must be supported through a transformation of how we think and how we interpret and value what we see and what we experience. To aid us in this struggle we have been given the mind of Christ (1Cor. 2:16)!

Salvation is experienced both as an event—a day, time, and place when we encounter Jesus Christ and undergo a new spiritual birth—and a process of sanctification, whereby we grow in the grace and knowledge of our Lord and Savior through exercising His mind and walking and warring in His power (2 Peter 3:18). While in the battle we are instructed to put on a spiritual helmet (mentioned three times, in Ephesians 6:17 and 1 Thessalonians 5:8, quoting Isaiah 59:17). The helmet is for protection of the mind so that we will not conform to the world's anti-God way of thinking. When Christians are unaware of the struggle being waged for human souls and do not guard their minds, they may become confused, dispirited, and ineffective, buffeted daily by ideas and values that are hostile to God and His rule. Passively allowing this present evil world to squeeze us into its mold is not what God had in mind for us when He provided such a great salvation!

Our inner life-force that is independent of the darkness ruling the world must be protected and nurtured to maintain a God-perspective on events, cultural trends, and socio-political developments. We apply caution (not fear!) to what we watch, what we read, what we hear; aided by the Word of God, by prayer and by Christian fellowship to open our eyes to God's ways and God's will, to keep us from becoming disoriented by spiritual warfare, and to encourage our obedience as we abandon our old thinking. The Apostle Paul was emphatic on the subject:

I beseech you therefore, brethren, by the mercies of God,
that ye present your bodies a living sacrifice, holy, acceptable unto God,
which is your reasonable service. And be not conformed to this world,

but be ye transformed by the renewing of your mind, that ye may prove what is that good, and acceptable, and perfect, will of God. (Romans 12:1-2)

A comparison between the old mind and the new mind will aid our understanding of the fight we are in.

THE REBELLIOUS MIND

1. ITS NATURE

   Those who have not been born again by the Spirit of God have the devil as their "father" and cannot know the truth (John 8:44). Before salvation, we are "dead" to the things of God (Ephesians 2:1), slaves to vain thinking, *having the understanding darkened, being alienated from the life of God (Ephesians 4:17-18),* blinded by the god of this world (2 Cor. 4:4), our minds corrupted (2 Timothy 3:8) and at enmity with God (Romans 8:7; Col. 1:21).

2. ITS MOTIVATION

   Impurity and unbelief (Titus 1:15), foolish pride (Romans 1:21-22; 1 Corinthians 1:18-29), and disobedience (1 Samuel 15:1-26). The dethronement of King Saul is particularly instructive as it illustrates the disastrous consequences of modifying God's commandments by our disobedient reasoning. Sadly, Christians can be equally guilty of pride and disobedience that produces doubt and disappointment contrary to the will of God.

3. ITS FRUIT

Alienation from God (1 Samuel 15:22-23) and judgment by God, who eventually gives up on those who persist in their sin and rebellion (Romans 1:18-32). The end is spiritual death, the wages of sin! (Romans 8:6a).

THE OBEDIENT MIND

1. ITS NATURE

Those who have been born again by the Spirit of God have "crucified the flesh" (including the mind) with its passions and desires. (Galatians 5:24). We are alive to God our Father, who puts His laws into our minds and writes them in our hearts. (Hebrews 8:10). We have the "mind of Christ" (1 Corinthians 2:16); it is a "sound mind" (2 Timothy 1:7).

2. ITS MOTIVATION

Love of God as a Heavenly Father is the primary motivation of a mind in submission to God: *Because ye are sons, God hath sent forth the Spirit of His Son into your hearts, crying Abba, Father (Gal. 4:6).* Other attributes flowing from *the love of God shed abroad in our hearts (Romans 5:5)* include simplicity and godly sincerity (2 Cor. 1:12), truth (2 Corinthians 4:2), humility (Philippians 2:1-8), purity (1 Timothy 1:5, 3:9), and transformation – a rejection of conformity to the world's thinking in favor of conformity to God's perfect will (Romans 12:1-2).

3. ITS FRUIT

Perfect peace (Isaiah 26:3; Philippians 4:7), sanctification (Ephesians 4:17-18, 22-24), wisdom, and prudence—the ability to govern oneself using reason (Ephesians 1:8-9).

The challenge for God's people who are always in the midst of spiritual battle is to be constantly reminded that swimming downstream is easy, but that is not our calling. We are obliged to swim against the powerful currents of wrong thinking, destructive beliefs, immoral values, and perverse activities that mark the world in which we live. However, we will drown if we attempt to do it on our own. We must learn to depend on the inner life of our conquering Savior, think as He thinks, and rest in His strength.

To paraphrase Moses and Joshua in their farewell speeches to the Israelites, we are to choose each day whom we will serve – the gods of this present evil world or *the King eternal, immortal, invisible, the* only wise God (1 Timothy 1:17).

CHAPTER FIVE

REMEMBER!

MEMORY IS A SIMPLE YET effective aid in the constant spiritual war against the deforming forces that target Christians in this present evil world. The battle waged by the enemy of our souls is fierce, but not unexpected. It is part of our spiritual training that helps to transform us from sinners into saints, ultimately to *conform* us to the image of Christ (Romans 8:29). Memories help to frame our responses and fuel our motivation during the change process—remembering who we were, where we came from, who we are now, how we got here, and where we are going reminds us why the struggle is important and worthwhile. Memories do not change the facts of our salvation, but they are vital to our continued spiritual growth.

Old Testament aids to remembering are linked to names and places and physical objects, monuments and memorials rich in allegorical content, primarily comprised of foundational materials such as rocks and stones, sculpted by God and not man. New Testament memorials are less tangible but no less powerful word pictures. In several important instances, Old Testament memorial events or physical objects are seen from a New Testament perspective as depicting deeply significant spiritual truths. The most notable example is the sacrificial lamb central to the first Passover in Egypt, a spectacular event preserved as an annual memorial:

The blood shall be unto you for a token [sign] upon the houses where you are,

> *and when I see the blood, I will pass over you, and the plague shall not be upon you*
> *to destroy you, when I smite the land of Egypt.*
> *And this day shall be unto you for a memorial,*
> *and ye shall keep it a feast to the Lord throughout your generations;*
> *ye shall keep it a feast by an ordinance forever (Exodus 12:13-14)*
> *Moses said unto the people,*
> *Remember this day in which ye came out from Egypt,*
> *out of the house of bondage, for by strength of hand*
> *the Lord brought you out from this place (Exodus 13:3)*
> *And thou shalt show thy son in that day, saying,*
> *This is done because of that which the Lord did unto me*
> *when I came out of Egypt (Exodus 13:8).*

The Passover memorial is elevated to a profound new level when the story is repeated in precise detail with the death of Jesus, the Lamb of God sacrificed not just as atonement for the sins of a single nation, but for the whole world. Christians memorialize the death, burial, and resurrection of Jesus in the solemn Communion Service, by replicating the essential elements of the so-called Last Supper or Lord's Supper (an echo of the Passover memorial), in accordance with His exhortation to His disciples, *This do in remembrance of me (Luke 22:19).*

Old Testament altars often served a dual purpose as both memorials and places of worship. The altars raised by Abraham at important stages of his journey are instructive. The first was when he arrived in Canaan (Genesis 12:7). After a brief sojourn in Egypt, he revisited the place of the first altar (Genesis 13:4). After separating from Lot, he settled in the plain of Mamre, and built an altar there (Genesis 13:18). His greatest altar was built for the sacrificing of his beloved son, an act of faith and obedience that led to the substitution of a ram for Isaac and the confirmation of God's covenant promise to Abraham. The entire episode recorded in Genesis 22:1-18 is a rich allegory that foreshadows the sacrifice of the Son of God almost 2,000 years in the future.

A key feature of Old Testament altars was their construction from stones that were not to be shaped by human hand. When Moses instructed the Israelites to build an altar for worship after entering the Promised Land (Deuteronomy 27:1-8) he specified the use of whole stones unmarked by any iron tools. Joshua later repeated this instruction (8:30-31). Much earlier in Israel's history Jacob's altar was a stone that he had used for a pillow (Gen. 28:10-22). The implication is clear. When we get involved in crafting an altar our professed focus on God tends to become a monument to our devotion and skills, as may be seen in any of the world's great cathedrals. Instead of being useful tools as gathering places for worshippers their intricate and extravagant beauty is a distraction that draws attention away from the One being worshipped to those who designed and built the place of worship. God does not favor competition. Through the mouths of His prophets, He condemns and mocks idols (Isaiah 46:5-9). In a New Testament description of the Body of Christ we see God reserving for Himself the job of molding us into a living temple. He builds altars for His glory, one rough stone at a time (1 Corinthians 12:18).

Stones used in the construction of monuments were treated differently. Monuments are for us, acting as markers for events that are important in our spiritual history. In the Old Testament, messages or reminders about the purpose of a monument would be cut into raw stone or into a covering of plaster. At the beginning of the story of the people of God in the Promised Land, stones taken from the bed of the river Jordan as they passed over on dry ground were piled on the bank of the river as a monument to the crossing (Joshua 4:1-8). In that case the intent was clear, and it applies equally in our day: When God picks us up from the mud beneath the river of sin, our life becomes a monument to His miraculous salvation and provision. All who meet us should be moved to ask: Who are you? Why are you different? What changed you?

It is important not only that our changed lives should be so noticeable as to attract attention from others, but also that we should frequently remind ourselves of how the change happened. When temptations or discouragements assail us, we are strengthened as we remember just how bad it was before we were saved and how great is that salvation!

Moses exhorted the Israelites to remember (Exodus 13:3) but they were disposed to forget and so they constantly complained and foolishly yearned for the "good old days." The litany of their moaning and groaning and harking back to a life that once enslaved them and caused them to beg God for deliverance is an embarrassing display of the fickle shallowness of the human heart that forgets so easily! (Exodus 2:23-24; 14:11-12; 16:2-3; 17:3; Numbers 11:4-6; 14:1-4; 20:2-5; 21:5).

Wandering for forty years in the wilderness was not necessary. It should have taken a few months at most to cover the distance of not more than 200 miles from Egypt to Canaan. Like those wandering Israelites, many Christians never seem to leave the wilderness and never experience a victorious Christian life, because they are not very familiar with God's Word and don't spend much time thinking about their walk with God. They become easy prey to heresies like the so-called "Prosperity Gospel" that declares they can claim all the milk and honey "by faith" in some formula that happily transforms God into a heavenly ATM machine. They forget who they are and where they came from and have little desire to learn anything more about God or about themselves. The journey from Exodus (enslaved by the god of this world) to Romans 8 (the victorious Christian life) is not that simple! But it is also not very complicated and will not take a lifetime if we learn from constant reference to God's Word and submit to Christ-centered preaching and fellowship in a local assembly of fellow-believers. Mature spiritual leaders and an under-shepherd dedicated to building Christ's Kingdom, not his own, are essential elements for rapid spiritual growth. Monuments to our progress are an aid to that end.

The closing chapter of the Promised Land conquest records a speech in which the Israelites are reminded about what God has done to bring them thus far. Joshua makes a covenant, raising a great stone as a witness (Joshua 24:26-27). The escape from slavery and settlement in the Promised Land was attended by numerous miracles. Our salvation and continuing walk with God are just as miraculous, and we continue to please Him by our ongoing consecration that invites Him to live through us. (See Romans 12:1-2.)

We draw strength in our walk with God by remembering! Above all, we should remember the day of our salvation, typified by the story of the Sacrificial Lamb and the Red Sea crossing, when we turned our back on the world. We remember also the day of our consecration, typified by the Jordan crossing, when we turned our back on our old self.

Inevitably, however, we will sometimes forget. Here is Charles Spurgeon's beautiful perspective on remembering and how God compensates for our forgetting (from "Morning and Evening"):

God does not say, "When ye shall look upon the rainbow, and ye shall remember my covenant, then

I will not destroy the earth," but it is gloriously put, not upon our memory, which is fickle and frail, but upon God's memory, which is infinite and immutable: "The bow shall be in the cloud; and I will look upon it, that I may remember the everlasting covenant." […] My looking to Jesus brings me joy and peace, but it is God's looking to Jesus which secures my salvation and that of all his elect, since it is impossible for our God to look at Christ, our bleeding Surety, and then to be angry with us for sins already punished in him […] We should remember the covenant, and we shall do it, through divine grace; but the hinge of our safety does not hang there—it is God's remembering us, not our remembering him; and hence the covenant is an everlasting covenant."

CHAPTER SIX

KEEPING THE SABBATH

TO UNDERSTAND THE MEANING AND importance of the Sabbath Rest for New Testament Christians it is necessary to go back to the Old Testament and consider the Sabbath Law that was part of the Ten Commandments (Exodus 20:8-11). Although Christians are not subject to the Law, we obey the commandments because they are universal moral standards—except the commandment about not working on a specific day.

Most Christians do not observe the Saturday Sabbath, seeing it as a purely Jewish law. Some Christian sects teach that keeping the seventh day Sabbath is essential to salvation, but this view not only reflects a fundamental misunderstanding of the meaning of our salvation in Jesus Christ but also ignores both the symbolism attached to that meaning, and actual New Testament practice.

Whenever Christ appears in His resurrected form and the

32

day is mentioned, it is always the first day of the week, Sunday (Matt. 28:1, 9, 10; Mark 16:9; Luke 24:1, 13, 15; John 20:19, 26). There is never any mention of Saturday gatherings for believers, but the first day of the week is mentioned in Acts 20:7 and 1 Corinthians 16:2. Sunday celebrates the New Creation with Christ as our resurrected head, and in the spirit of that new creation, as those who are alive from the dead (Romans 6:13), whose lives are not our own (1 Corinthians 6:20), we are to worship God every day, not just on a particular day. On the other hand, we do need to set aside a day to gather for corporate worship, and by general consent, that day is Sunday.

One practical reason why the first Christians met on Sunday was that many of them would have attended synagogues or the Temple on Saturday! The first few years after the birth of the church were a transition period when many Christians struggled to come to terms with their new faith. They saw themselves as Jews first and had only the Hebrew (Old Testament) Scriptures for reference. Galatians 4 has a useful summary of the resulting tensions, and Colossians 2:16-23 answers some questions regarding Jewish observances, including the Sabbath.

However, despite the evidence indicating that Christians are not obliged to keep the Saturday Sabbath, we cannot overlook the fact that God draws attention to resting on the seventh day of Creation. The all-powerful God could have created the universe in seven seconds, yet He chose to do it in seven days, with the seventh day demarcated as a rest day, a day to cease from working. Scripture tells us that God not only stopped working on the seventh day but that He blessed it and set it apart (made it holy, Genesis 2:2-3) as a day for rest from ordinary labor, a day for spiritual service, a day that belonged to Him. It is significant that this rest day was also the first full day for Adam and Eve after their creation on the sixth day. Almighty, omnipotent God did not need the rest! It was for those who serve Him.

The requirement was so important that it was the first commandment to be observed by His people, even before the Law was given. In the Exodus account the Israelites gathered manna sent from heaven as daily bread to feed them. They were not to try and store it but to eat it all each day. If they tried to live on today's bread tomorrow, it would turn rotten. The picture for us could not be more explicit: Our daily bread is to eat of God's Word each day and to nurture the life of Christ within us through daily prayer. We must not try to live today on yesterday's blessings! The exception for the Israelites was the sixth day, when they gathered a double portion of manna to feed them on the seventh day, their day of rest. The full story is told in Exodus 16:4-5; 14-26.

The Sabbath rest is formally included in the list of Ten Commandments given to the Hebrews a little later (Exodus 20:8-11). In all, it is mentioned 30 times in the Books of Moses, more than any other commandment. The penalty for breaking this commandment, even in the smallest way, was severe and final: death by stoning! (Numbers 15:32-36). This harsh penalty focuses our attention on both the importance of gathering heavenly bread each day, and of resting on one special day to focus on God alone.

Our relationship with God as New Testament Christians places an entirely new emphasis on "a day of rest" that would have been inconceivable to Old Testament Israelites. In the New Testament context of salvation, we are spiritually dead until we "keep" the Sabbath by resting in Jesus! The letter to the Hebrews clearly outlines this principle in chapters three and four. The writer refers to Psalm 95:7-11 in exhorting his Jewish readers not to repeat the rebellion of their ancestors who failed to enter the Promised Land, but to partake of Christ, who is our Promised Land! (Note that "Jesus" in verse 8 is a translation from New Testament Greek; the Old Testament Hebrew version of this name is Joshua).

"Rest" is mentioned ten times from Hebrews 3:11 to 4:11. Chapter 4:8-10 is a reference to salvation by faith and not works (Ephesians 2:8-9). To sum up: We see God resting after His labors in Creation as an example to the Israelites to rest from their labors on the seventh day Sabbath. It is also a message to all seekers after God to rest permanently from their dead works by placing their faith in Christ. Clearly, the Old Testament Sabbath was not an end but pointed forward to a vital principle that would be revealed in the sacrifice of Jesus Christ: for everyone seeking reconciliation with God, when Jesus cried, "It is finished!" (John 19:30) as He died on the cross, His work of salvation was complete. There is now nothing left for us to do—not one, little, thing—to save ourselves. God requires only that we rest in what He has done. When we come empty-handed to God, and by faith, not our work, receive salvation in Jesus Christ, we enter an eternal Sabbath rest. If you are saved, you are a Sabbath keeper in Christ; if you are not saved, it matters not what else you are, you are doomed!

The principle of resting from our labors of self-justification and self-promotion and self-protection is vital for our salvation if we are to live a victorious and spiritually productive Christian life. The principle is illustrated again and again throughout Scripture, that God does not require us to sweat for Him but submit to Him! There was an occasion in Israel's history when they were leaving Egypt on their way to the Promised Land: ahead was the impenetrable barrier of the Red Sea, behind was the might of the pursuing Egyptian army. The people cried out in terror. Then Moses spoke—he who had learned something about trusting God during his 40-year apprenticeship as a humble wilderness shepherd:

Fear ye not, stand still, and see the salvation of the Lord. (Exodus 14:13)

The people stopped running and trusted God. They could not imagine what He would do next, but instead of looking at the threat behind them, they looked up. Then the sea parted. A great deliverance took place. *Stand still!* The command of God has not changed in 4,000 years. *Stand. Still!* Look up. Wait. God is in control. Scripture declares:

Behold, I lay in Zion for a foundation a stone, a tried stone,
a precious corner stone, a sure foundation;
he that believeth shall not make haste.
(Isaiah 28:16)

Not making haste means not acting independent of God, not doing what you think is best. That is the way of sweat and stress and anxiety and uncertainty. The results are always, sooner or later, disastrous. The identical thought carries through to the New Testament where Paul's classic exposition on spiritual warfare warns us that in our battle against "the rulers of the darkness of this world" we are to make use of the whole armor of God,

That ye may be able to withstand in the evil day,
and having done all, to stand.
Stand therefore...
(Ephesians 6:13-14)

When you learn to stand, it brings rest:

Come unto me, all ye that labor and are heavy laden,
and I will give you rest. Take my yoke upon you, and learn of me;
for I am meek and lowly in heart:
and ye shall find rest unto your souls.
(Matthew 11:28-30)

Note that the first rest (verse 28) is a gift: the gift of salvation. But entering into the second rest takes work! When our burden of sin is lifted, and we experience the rest of salvation, Jesus immediately offers us the burden of service (a yoke) through which we learn to find rest. But how is it possible to rest while working? The answer to this question goes to the very heart of the Christian experience. Misunderstanding dooms many sincere Christians to lives that are a burden to themselves and unsatisfactory to God because our idea of work and God's idea of work bear no resemblance to each other.

Work to us denotes labor and the expectation of some reward for our efforts. When the anticipated payoff doesn't come, we grow impatient and dissatisfied. This is not the work that Jesus means. His work is spiritual; the service He has in view is service *to* Him, and *with* Him, not *for* Him. Alas, we are often so entrenched in our idea of work and so confident of our natural abilities that it is difficult to appreciate what Jesus is calling us to do. Yet we must see it if we are to grow spiritually, if we are ever to liberate ourselves from the tyranny of cluttered schedules and crushing workloads and the impatience and disappointment that is fueled by unmet deadlines and unfulfilled expectations.

According to Matthew 11:28-30, finding rest in the midst of busyness simply requires us to follow our Savior's invitation to yoke up with Him. We may appreciate the full impact of the invitation by imagining that we are a little beast of burden (a donkey, perhaps) yoked alone to a very heavy load. The task is difficult, and we are soon exhausted and discouraged. Then the great and infinitely powerful God comes alongside and gently says, "Take my yoke upon you! Let me share the load with you." Let that thought sink in and then consider that it is no burden to stand in God's presence, awed by His beauty and holiness and love. In fact, He demands that we approach Him with empty hands, an empty agenda, an empty "Do List" and a blank personal performance checklist:

They shall come near to me to minister unto me,
and they shall stand before me to offer unto me the fat and the blood,
saith the Lord God. They shall enter into my sanctuary,
and they shall come near to my table,
to minister unto me, and they shall keep my charge.
They shall not gird themselves with anything that causeth sweat.
(Ezekiel 44:15-16, 18)

This all-important principle is graphically illustrated in the story of Mary and Martha told in Luke 10:38-42. Here we see Martha distracted by her tasks in the kitchen as she worked *for* Jesus. Her motives were pure—she wanted to be a blessing to her beloved Friend. Her sister Mary, on the other hand, expressed her service *to* Jesus by sitting motionless at His feet, hanging on His every word, learning from Him, enjoying His Presence. Jesus said she chose the better part!

The great missionary to China, Hudson Taylor, aptly summarized the idea of resting in God:

Bear not a single care thyself,
One is too much for thee;

39

The work is mine, and mine alone;
Thy work - to rest in me."

The most telling outward characteristics of a Christian should be joy and peace (or rest). Before you become aware of the beliefs of others we will notice their joy and peace flowing from reconciliation both with God and to the circumstances of their life.

Someone has said that God's will is exactly what we would choose if we had all the facts. After salvation, resting in God is believing that we abide in the One who does have all the facts, and trusting Him to work circumstances according to His perfect will regardless of what temporal events or our physical senses tell us. This is the way of peace, a sure antidote to impatience or fear.

Just rest in Him! Keep the Sabbath!

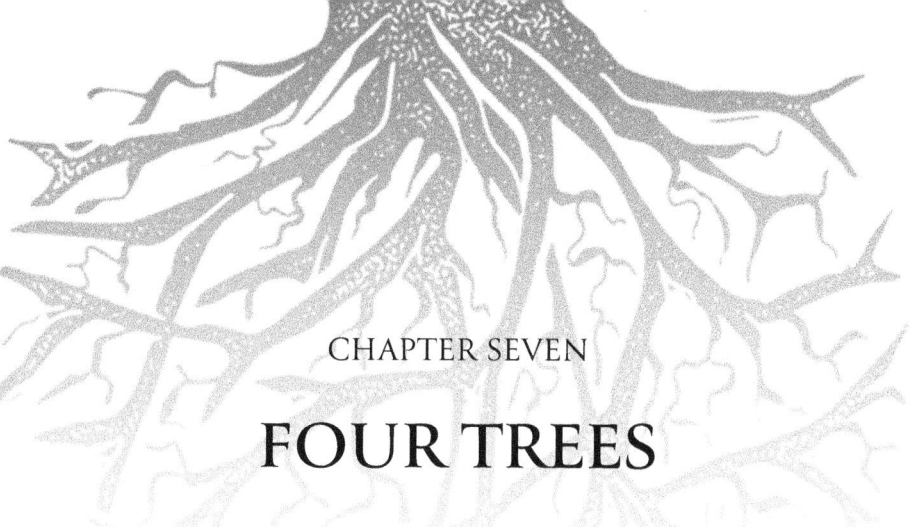

CHAPTER SEVEN

FOUR TREES

IN OUR STUDY OF BIBLICAL allegories, we are discovering that the Bible's spiritually rich pages contain many treasures to edify, teach, instruct, and direct God's people. Characters, circumstances, themes, patterns, parables, allegories, names, places, and events all combine in a rich tapestry to enlighten us and bring us closer to conformity with God's will.

Nothing is wasted. There is no accident about the way in which the Bible is constructed. Even the smallest facts and events have meaning: the challenge to the reader is to extract the rich ore of spiritual knowledge and instruction from the mine of truth found on every page. We must never fall into the habit of ignoring Scripture passages that we don't understand. "That makes no sense!" is a thought that should alert us to dig deeper. If we are wise, we will pause to learn the meaning, while fools skip ahead and continue in their ignorance.

In the previous chapter we explored what it means to "Keep the Sabbath" and discovered that in the New Testament context

41

of salvation, we are spiritually dead until we enter into a Sabbath Rest with Jesus our Savior. In this chapter we are going to focus on trees. Specifically, four trees are in view as identified by references in Genesis, Psalms, Galatians, and Revelation. The trees are each unique, yet related; they each have an allegorical story to tell that forms part of a greater whole.

TWO TREES PLANTED BY GOD
GENESIS 2:9,16-17; 3:5-6,17

The Tree of Life
- Its fruit is unappreciated
- There are no restrictions to eating its fruit
- The fruit is accessible through our obedience
- Obedience leads to life

The Tree of Knowledge of Good and Evil
- Its fruit is desirable
- Its fruit is forbidden
- Satan tempts man to eat of it
- Disobedience and eating brings a curse, and death

A TREE PLANTED BY MAN
GALATIANS 3:13

The Tree of Judgment
- Only fallen man could fashion and plant such a cruel tree

- It is a tree of judgment and of suffering
- It grows out of man's rejection of the Tree of Life
- Everything associated with the judgment tree speaks of death, and its fruit is hideous (*Psalm 22:6-17*). When Adam and Eve so readily ate the forbidden fruit, they could not have imagined the horrifying chain of events their disobedience would unleash on the world.
- The judgment tree forever epitomizes the sadistic torture and death of our Creator in human form, who died to pay for the sins of Adam and Eve, and our sins.
- Nobody who was hung on the judgment tree ever escaped. Jesus was no different. The only way out was death.
- When Jesus died, darkness fell on the earth to cloak the awful sight of His body torn apart, scarred and deformed by our sin. Yet by His death He brought forth new life!

A TREE PLANTED BY JESUS CHRIST
PSALM 1:1-3; REVELATION 22:1-5

Adam and Eve had access to everything in the Garden of Eden, especially access to God who walked and talked with them each day (and went looking for them when they hid from Him because of their sin). Only the fruit of one tree

43

was denied them, and they lost everything because they ate that one forbidden fruit.

Now we who are descendants of Adam and Eve may be restored to fellowship with God in only one way: by eating the fruit of the Tree of Life!

The Tree of Resurrection Life

- When the fruit died on the Tree of Judgment it was buried.

- Then it sprang into new life as a living tree bearing living fruit

- Satan fights to prevent us from eating of this life-giving tree

- Eating brings eternal life. All that was lost in Eden is restored

- The tree is eternally watered and protected by a river of life

- It is fruitful, and reproduces itself (*Psalm 92:12-14* with *Proverbs 11:30—the fruit of the righteous is a tree of life*)

- It is a new creation of God: new life in a new world where every tongue confesses the Lordship of Jesus Christ (*Revelation 5:8-14*)

As the last Adam, Christ is the sum of all failed humanity—as the second Man He is the head of a victorious new race. (1 Corinthians 15:45). Having in His death done away with the first man in whom God's purpose was frustrated, Jesus rose again to ensure God's purpose would be forever fruitful—not by religion but by revelation; not by application but by inspiration; not by education but by *life*. The supernatural life of Christ which becomes ours at salvation ensures that we in turn become living trees watered eternally by a river of life.

Chinese Christian teacher Watchman Nee observed that we are not educated to become Christians, because God's children are born, not taught! On the other hand, we must be taught to become spiritually mature Christians.

Christ is our life. He lives out His life in us and through us . As such, He is both the Giver and the Gift of Life, a River of Life, and a magnificent Healing Tree on the banks of that River. He is also the fruit of the tree and the seed in the fruit that brings forth life in you and me!

The Apostle Paul said it best in his letter to the Colossians: Christ is all, and in all, and we are complete in Him (Col. 2:10 & 3:11).

The challenge to us who have eaten of that living fruit and drank of that living water is to live our new life as a clear declaration that we are no longer a part of the old creation; no longer open to the devil's lies, tempted again and again to eat forbidden fruit and seeking fulfillment in things that produce death, not life—the lust of the flesh (what makes us feel good), the lust of the eyes (looking beyond our needs, to satisfy our wants), and the pride of life (seeking a place in life beyond what Jesus calls us to be—bondservants, willing slaves to Him).

As new creations in Jesus Christ, everything is new, and whole, and good, and eternal, planted beside an always flowing river of life and reproducing the Life in others.

CHAPTER EIGHT

TWO BRIDES

OF ALL THE RICH ALLEGORIES in Scripture none bares the heart of God more than the word pictures He draws of His passionate love for us and intimate relationship with us. It is a narrative both heartbreaking and hart-warming as it unveils the depths of our corruption and un-loveliness and underlines His persistent wooing and loving.

It is not an easy story to read. Scripture is unsparing in its honest depiction of us; things we would rather not speak of, nor acknowledge about ourselves. We are born slaves to sin, and sin knows no boundaries. Even after our salvation the habit of sin remains strong. We bring that bad habit with us in our relationship with God as He builds the church, the Body of Christ, one saved sinner at a time.

It is, however, from such unpromising clay that His glory is revealed on earth (Ephesians 3:21) and His wisdom becomes known to principalities and powers in heavenly places (Ephesians 3:9-10). In the end, because—thankfully—God is God

46

and nothing can deter Him from His purpose, we are made altogether lovely, a fitting heavenly partner for our Redeemer. Our biography begins in Genesis where our downfall is recorded, and we are revealed as rebellious and disobedient sinners. But the story ends gloriously in John's Revelation where we appear as a glittering Bride to a Holy and Majestic King of Kings.

There are three parts to the story: our personal biography, our biography as a sinful earthly bride (where we are now), and finally, our future as the perfect Bride of Christ.

OUR PERSONAL BIOGRAPHY
RUIN, REDEMPTION, RELAPSE, RESTORATION

A single act of unthinking disobedience by the first human couple, recorded in the third chapter of Genesis, brought immediate ruin to what God had just pronounced "very good." The story from there traces the downfall of each new generation of persistent sinners. Most books of the Bible, both Old and New Testaments, tell in varying degrees of detail about sinners born as cast-offs from the family of God, and the effects of their sinfulness. None does it better that the Prophet Ezekiel, especially in a single astounding chapter 16 that depicts our ruin, redemption, relapse, and ultimate glorious restoration.

The story begins with the horrifying depiction of a newborn child, abandoned, unlovely, and helpless (Ezekiel 16:1-5). The child is us, born slaves to sin until God rescues us, cleans us, loves, and beautifies us—(Ezekiel 16:6-14). Then, rejoicing in our new life we inevitably play the harlot, selling ourselves and all God's gifts to any sin that will have us (Ezekiel 16:15-22, 30, 33). God promises to deal with our sinfulness (Ezekiel. 16:59).

Then, incredibly, He declares that He is willing to restore us, leaving us speechless with shame at our wretched unworthiness in the presence of His great love (Ezekiel 16:60-63).

OUR BIOGRAPHY AS A SINFUL EARTHLY BRIDE

FAITHLESSNESS TO GOD WHO REMAINS FOREVER FAITHFUL AS WE MAKE OUR WAY IN THIS LIFE.

The incarnate God purchased the Church with His own blood—Acts 20:28. In Ephesians 5:25-27 we learn that Christ gave Himself for the church to make it glorious! But as we have noted, the church is made up of sinful individuals. The Prophet Hosea (1:2-3) illustrates our transition from individuals to a collective Body that remains sinful in its individual parts.

When our sinful lusts cause us to desert Him, God buys us back and demands that we remain faithful to Him because He paid so much for us—Hosea 3:1-3. At last, we find deliverance in His persistent love—Hosea 13:9; 14:4,8

OUR FUTURE AS THE PERFECT BRIDE OF CHRIST

A GRACEFUL BRIDEGROOM AND A GLORIOUS DESTINY AWAIT US IN HEAVEN

Psalm 45 (especially verses 10 to 17) is an allegory about the Bride of Christ, the Church, the daughter of the great King. It presents the first complete picture of what God has in mind for those whom He redeems. Other Scriptures fill in the details.

a. Isaiah 54:5 identifies God as both our maker and our husband.

b. The Song of Solomon (especially 2:1-12) presents another extended allegory, in the form of a passionate love poem typical of the time in which it was written, of the fervent love between Christ and His bride.

c. John 3:28-29 identifies Jesus as the Bridegroom, with John the Baptist speaking as the best man at His wedding.

d. Revelation 19:6-9 describes the heavenly marriage supper

e. Revelation 21:1-5 reveals the Church, the Bride, as the New Jerusalem in a new heaven and a new earth

f. Revelation 22:16-17 presents a final invitation to join this perfect spiritual union in heaven.

Only God could imagine such a story. Only God could write it not at fantasy but as fact.

We who are fortunate participants in that story appear alongside heroes like Abraham and Sarah and Moses and Rahab and Gideon and Samson and King David and others whose triumphs of faith are recorded in Hebrews 11. There is no record of their failures! The glorious truth is that their sinful deeds are forever washed away in the Blood of the Lamb and all that remains is the good that they did.

The eternal sacrificial Lamb is also the Lion of the tribe of Judah, the mighty King who loves us with an everlasting love and gave Himself for us so that we could live forever in glory with Him.

The challenge for us today is to show ourselves worthy of such great love by serving our Lord and Savior Jesus Christ with a true heart and a clear conscience as we make our way through this present evil world.

CHAPTER NINE

FROM MARITAL CHAOS
TO WEDDED BLISS

*WHEN DIVORCE AND RE-MARRIAGE
IS A GOOD THING!*

MARRIAGES AS GOD DESIGNED THEM are complex relationships between two very different people – a man and a woman. The marriage story begins with Adam & Eve, who were wedded to each other—and to God. But the first couple chose to disobey their Creator and their sin led to separation from God. The marital chaos that followed that first fatal sin is evident to this day. Strife, betrayal and heartbreak, multiple divorces and remarriages are commonplace and there is no shame in rampant infidelity outside of marriage. It is a testimony to the world's marriage to sin and separation from God, who views all sin as spiritual adultery.

The biblical way to avoid such adulterous behavior is to

51

"divorce" from its source, that is, from this present evil world, our corrupt old nature, and the depraved adversarial spirit constantly focused on luring us away from God. See Ezra chapters 9-10, especially 10:10-11:

And Ezra the priest stood up, and said unto them,
Ye have transgressed, and have taken strange wives,
to increase the trespass of Israel.
Now therefore make confession unto the LORD God of your fathers,
and do his pleasure: and separate yourselves from the people of the land,
and from the strange wives.

A powerful allegory illustrating the foolish and destructive nature of sin when we are married to it is found in 1 Samuel 25, the story of Abigail and David. The story is about a man, Nabal (whose name means "fool" and who is described as "churlish" – rude and impolite), who needlessly antagonizes David. His wife is named Abigail, which means "the joy of her father". Abigail's swift action turns aside David's wrath against Nabal, who soon dies of a heart attack, leaving Abigail free to marry David. The story is wonderfully summarized in a single sentence spoken by Abigail to David:

A man is risen to pursue thee, and to seek thy soul,
but the soul of my Lord shall be bound in the bundle of life
with the Lord thy God;
and the souls of thine enemies, them shall He sling out (1 Samuel 25:29).

Separation from foolish worldliness and faithful marriage to

52

God is seen throughout Scripture as a defining characteristic of sincere Christians. We will take a brief look at the Principles, the Purpose and the Power of Separation as presented in several New Testament passages.

THE PRINCIPLES OF SEPARATION

GOD COMMANDS IT (2 CORINTHIANS 6:14-17)

> *Be yet not unequally yoked together with unbelievers:*
> *for what fellowship hath righteousness with unrighteousness?*
> *And what communion hath light with darkness?*
> *And what concord hath Christ with Belial?*
> *Or what part hath he that believeth with an infidel?*
> *And what agreement hath the temple of God with idols?*
> *For ye are the temple of the living God, as God hath said,*
> *I will dwell in them, and walk in them, and I will be their God,*
> *and they shall by my people.*
> *Wherefore come out from among them, and be ye separate,*
> *saith the Lord, and touch not the unclean thing,*
> *and I will receive you, and will be a Father unto you, and*
> *ye shall be my sons and daughters, saith the Lord Almighty.*

LOVE DEMANDS IT (1 JOHN 2:15)

> *Love not the world, neither the things that are in the world.*
> *If any man love the world, the love of the Father is not in him.*

CITIZENSHIP REQUIRES IT (COLOSSIANS 1:12-13)

> *Giving thanks unto the Father which hath made us meet*

to be partakers of the inheritance of the saints in light:
who hath delivered us from the power of darkness,
and hath translated us into the kingdom of His dear Son.

THE PURPOSE OF SEPARATION

We are separated to be sanctified: First, we leave "Egypt" (an allegorical picture of this present evil world system to which we are bound as slaves by sin), and then sanctification follows—*Exodus 19:1-11* and *James 4:4*.

Note that sanctification is not an end in itself! We remain on earth after salvation because God desires that we share the Gospel with others, and we need His Power to fulfill His Purpose. When Jesus' *called* His disciples, He did not say, "Follow me and I will make you holy."

Follow me and I will make you fishers of men (Matthew 4:19)

When Jesus *commissioned* His disciples to be soul-winners, He provided His power for them to do so.

All power is given unto me in heaven and in earth.
Go ye therefore, and teach all nations, baptizing them
In the name of the Father, and of the Son, and of the Holy Ghost.
(Matthew 28:18-19)

THE POWER OF SEPARATION

The Lever Principle

The ancient Greek mathematician Archimedes famously

said, "Give me a lever long enough and a fulcrum on which to place it, and I can move the world."

Christians have been given a mighty fulcrum—God's Word. All we need in addition to that is Christians who will stand so far away from this present evil world that they can move it! When we separate ourselves from the world and sanctify ourselves to God, we can expect to experience God's power to do God's will.

Joshua said unto the people, Sanctify yourselves,
for tomorrow the Lord will do wonders among you.
(Joshua 3:5)

In the Old Testament God's power was necessary to win wars and subdue kingdoms. In the N.T. it is necessary to liberate sinners from the kingdom of darkness.

Jesus returned in the power of the Spirit into Galilee: and there went out a fame of Him through all the region round about. (See Luke 4:14-19)

The "power of the Spirit" is available only to those who recognize their need for it, turn their backs on the world to receive it, and then ask God for it. It would revolutionize the life of every Christian if we saw our relationship with God as something worth cleaving to, "forsaking all others". Think of that the next time you are tempted by some "little sin", or tempted to compromise your principles, or tempted to adopt some worldly fad or point of view. Or better yet, fall so deeply in love with Jesus that you don't even notice temptations and distractions because you have eyes only for Him!

CHAPTER TEN

PROFILES IN PERSONAL EVANGELISM

*HE THAT WINNETH SOULS IS WISE
(PROVERBS. 11:30)*

IN BOTH THE OLD TESTAMENT and New Testament
God's people are required to witness to others: in the Old
Testament it was the nation of Israel; in the New Testament
it is each local church. In both cases, individuals within those
bodies are the actual bearers of God's message.

When Jesus came to earth, He declared that He was empowered by God to "seek and to save that which was lost." (Luke
19:10). Then He declared His purpose for us: *Follow me, and I
will make you fishers of men.* (Matthew 4:19). He also revealed the
essential ingredient in soulwinning: *It is the Spirit that quickeneth*
[gives life]; *the flesh profiteth nothing: the words that I speak unto you,
they are spirit, and they are life.* (John 6:63).

The Apostle Paul echoed his Savior's words in declaring:
My speech and my preaching was not with enticing words of man's

wisdom, but in demonstration of the Spirit and power, that your faith should not stand in the wisdom of men, but in the power of God. (1 Corinthians 2:4-5).

Clearly, we must have God's power to do God's work. The allegory of the Valley of Dry Bones outlined in Ezekiel 37:1-10 is a vivid picture of what it takes to revive those who are spiritually dead. We can further aid our efforts to become fishers of men (and women! and children!) by learning from many rich soul winning allegories in Scripture. Each highlights a different aspect of personal evangelism. Each tells a story that we may relate to from our own experience. Here are a few examples:

THE IMPACT OF A DEVOTED WOMAN

The story of Naomi teaches that godly character may have a strong influence on those who are close to us. The key passage in Ruth 1:14-17 is a is a powerful testimony from a former unbeliever to Naomi's character and the reality of her God.

> *Whither thou goest, I will go.*
> *And where thou lodgest, I will lodge.*
> *Thy people shall be my people,*
> *And thy God, my God.*

LOVING THE UNLOVELY

A man made rotten by sin and rejected by all is transformed

by the touch of a personal evangelist. The story in Matthew 8:1-3 demonstrates that Jesus never hesitated to reach out even to those whom it was forbidden to touch.

And behold, there came a leper and worshipped Him,
Saying, Lord, if thou wilt, thou canst make me clean.
And Jesus put forth His hand, and touched him,
Saying, I will; be thou clean.
And immediately his leprosy was cleansed.

CONVERSION BRINGS CONTROVERSY (AND HOW TO HANDLE IT!)

A man who knew nothing, knew the only thing that matters! (John 9:8-25). The story rewards careful study because it is packed with details reflecting the priorities or prejudices of the different characters—from the blind beggar who represents every penitent sinner; his mystified and compromising parents; the offended religious scholars who disdain the beggar's ignorance; and the personal evangelist who takes time to establish the man in his faith after his sight is restored.

The best line in the story comes from the mouth of the beggar who is unqualified to debate his detractors but is happy to declare an indisputable fact: "Once I was blind, but now I see!"

THE WORST SINNERS SOMETIMES MAKE THE BEST CONVERTS

Lessons from two sinful women whose response to Jesus was driven by their spiritual thirst and elevated by their joyful gratitude. Their stories are told in Luke 7:36-50 and John 4:7-42.

A SOUL WINNING STORY THAT HAS EVERYTHING!

Conversion. Consternation. Consecration and Communication.

A man rejected for his madness and then rejected for his wholeness, becomes an evangelist to his community! (Luke 8:26-39).

ARE YOU A PERSONAL EVANGELIST?

You should be able to see yourself in one of these word pictures and be encouraged and inspired by them. If you do not find them interesting and informative, it may be that you are not saved and don't understand what all the fuss is about. Alternatively, you are not yet a committed "soulwinner".

From the emphasis Scripture gives to sharing our faith with others it is clearly something God wants to make a practical and constant part of our lives. But many Christians pretend it is an optional requirement. Others shrug it off as something the pastor is paid to do. In either case, we rob ourselves of great spiritual blessings and benefits when we fail to "go and tell". A commitment to sharing our faith means that we get to know our Bible a lot better so that we can both share the

Gospel and answer questions about scriptural passages that some might find difficult to understand. Another great benefit is that we will get to know ourselves a lot better! Just how deep is our walk with God? How obedient are we? How do we handle stress that comes from approaching complete strangers with the Gospel message? How do we share our faith with close friends and family members! And how much do we really care that people all around us are like the walking dead, stumbling blindly towards eternal darkness? Perhaps, like the unfortunate father who begged Jesus to heal his tormented son we should cry out, *Lord, I believe; help thou mine unbelief!"* (Mark 9:24)

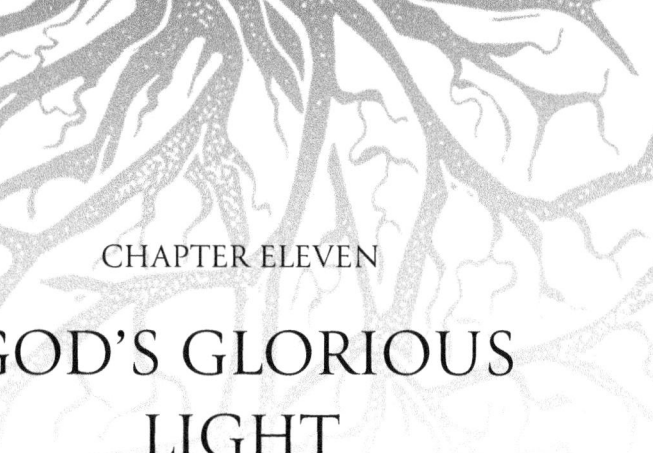

CHAPTER ELEVEN

GOD'S GLORIOUS LIGHT

In the beginning God created the heavens and the earth
And the earth was without form, and void,
and darkness was upon the face of the deep.
And the Spirit of God moved upon the face of the waters.
And God said, "Let there be light."
And there was light. Genesis 1:1-3

IMAGINE WHAT IT WAS LIKE on the first day of Creation, and on each subsequent day, especially the fourth day and the sixth day and then on the fateful day when Adam and Eve sinned. In the beginning of Creation God spoke light into the darkness even before creating, on the fourth day, sources of earthly light in the sun, moon, and stars. On the sixth day He created Adam and Eve, specifically to reflect His own unique light that shone brighter than any star.

God's light is an allegorical picture of God Himself – brilliant in purity and in power, and glorious in opposition to both natural

61

darkness and spiritual darkness which must always flee from the mere hint of light's presence. Darkness is an allegorical picture of sin in the absence of God and His Light. Satan, the parent of sin, is described as the ruler of the darkness of this world (Ephesians 6:12). That darkness entered through the two first humans who were the crowning glory of God's Creation, made in His image. Had they not taken the forbidden fruit, but had eaten instead from the Tree of Life, they and their descendants would have reflected God's divine light forever.

But they disobeyed. All they knew up to that moment was sunlight and moonlight and starlight and God's light and they did not appreciate God's light as something very different from the created sources of light. When darkness entered again in the instant they disobeyed, it brought something new into the world. On the first day of Creation there was merely the absence of visible light; now there was the absence of the Lightbringer, and the darkness was not around them, but in them. Scripture refers to the darkness when God withdraws His light from the presence of sin as "thick darkness". It is darkness that He wears like a cloak, as a barrier against sin. In Exodus 20:21, when God prepares to reveal His Law, we learn that "the people stood afar off, and Moses drew near to the thick darkness where God was." Psalm 18:11 declares: "He made darkness His secret place".

This was the legacy of Adam and Eve's sin. Instead of appearing as Light, God was now darkness to them and to all their descendants. It seemed His purpose had been defeated. But the Gospel assures us the initial appearance of defeat was not the end of the story. The Creator's wisdom, foresight and power had something much greater in mind: He would renew the light and banish the darkness forever in a spectacular way that only He could conceive. When God first brought the light, it was a physical manifestation that He spoke into existence. Now, out of the spiritual darkness and chaos that resulted from the fall of man, God would bring forth the glorious light of His own presence and power, *in* man, and *through* man. The object of God's apparent great defeat by Satan would be a vessel to fully display God's glory, made greater still by its appearance out of such dark clay. We would not merely reflect His light but be bearers of it, and co-creators of more light by sharing the Good News with others!

God's light in us, working a transformation like the first day of Creation, begins whenever a lost soul turns to God and receives salvation. It is an extraordinary event, described in brief outline by the Apostle Paul:

God who commanded the light to shine out of darkness
hath shined in our hearts
to give the light of the knowledge of the glory of God
in the face of Jesus Christ.
But we have this treasure in earthen vessels,
that the excellency of the power may be of God,
and not of us.
(2 Corinthians 4:6-7)

The opening to the Gospel of John introduces this amazing plan by declaring:

In Him was Life; and the Life was the light of men.
And the light shineth in darkness [...]
That was the true Light which lighteth
every man that cometh into the world [...]
As many as received Him, to them gave he power
to become the sons of God.
(John 1:4-5; 9,12)

The Gospel later shares this prayer of Jesus about us:

That they all may be one,
as thou, Father, art in me, and I in thee,
that they may also be one in us, that the world may believe
that thou hast sent me.
And the glory which thou gavest me
I have given them... (John 17:21-22)

Adam could not have imagined the unfolding revelation of God's purpose when he was banished from Eden. He had known the Light and did not appreciate it. Then darkness became his companion and he longed for the Light but did not know how or where to find it. Adam could not have understood how his descendants born into his spiritual darkness would become beneficiaries of his fall. We have received a book that teaches us about God and the magnificent story of His redemption plan, drawing us to His Light that is such a brilliant contrast to our experience of darkness. The Old Testament begins the story by introducing God's Creation Light and recording the vast consequences of Adam's sin. The New Testament adds the possibility of Light's location within us, through redemption in Christ. The complete picture reveals God's intention to banish darkness forever, unveiling Himself in and through a spiritual Body of Christ—redeemed individuals, each bearing His Light, then uniting and multiplying His unrestrained glory. Scripture methodically develops this story of emerging Light.

GLORY IN THE OLD TESTAMENT TAB-ERNACLE AND TEMPLE

Exodus 25: 1-8 contains instructions for building the first Tabernacle after the escape from Egypt: *And let them make me a sanctuary, that I may dwell amongst them (25:8)*

Exodus 40:1-33 gives instructions for assembling the tabernacle. Exodus 40:34 records what happened when the tabernacle was ready: *Then a cloud covered the tent of the congregation, and the glory of the Lord filled the tabernacle*

Leviticus 9:22-24 records the moment when the sacrifices were made ready in the tabernacle and God's power entered:

And there came a fire out from before the Lord,
and consumed upon the altar the burnt offering and the fat:
which when all the people saw, they shouted, and fell on their faces

I Kings 8:10-11 records the completion of Solomon's great Temple that replaced the tabernacle:

And it came to pass, when the priests were come

out of the holy place, that the cloud filled the house of the Lord,

so that the priests could not minister because of the cloud:

For the glory of the Lord had filled the house of the Lord.

2 Chronicles 7:1-2 echoes the account in Leviticus when the sacrifices were made ready in the Temple and God's power entered:

The fire came down from heaven and consumed the burnt offering

and the sacrifices; and the glory of the Lord filled the house.

And the priests could not enter into the house of the Lord,

because the glory of the Lord had filled the Lord's house.

GLORY IN THE NEW TESTAMENT TEMPLE

Isaiah 60:1-3 refers specifically to Christ, but in a New Testament context the words could equally apply to the church, the Body of Christ.

Arise, shine for thy light is come, and the glory of the Lord is risen upon thee. For behold, the darkness shall cover the earth, and gross darkness the people: but the Lord shall arise upon thee, and His glory shall be seen upon thee. And the Gentiles shall come to thy light, and kings to the brightness of thy rising.

Isaiah 66:1-2The prophet expands on the thought of God seeking a new kind of Temple when He proclaims:

Thus saith the Lord, The heaven is my throne

and the earth is my footstool: where is the house that ye build unto me?
And where is the place of my rest?
For all these things hath my hand made,
and all these things have been, saith the Lord.
But to this man will I look,
even to him that is poor and of a contrite spirit, and trembles at my word.

I Corinthians 3:16 — Paul confirms that God now resides in a Temple not made with hands!

Know ye not that ye are the Temple of God,
and that the Spirit of God dwelleth in you?

2 Corinthians 6:16

Ye are the temple of the living God; as God hath said,
I will dwell in them, and walk in them,
and I will be their God, and they shall be my people.

Ephesians 1:18-19 — Paul prays for us to understand God's purpose for us; God's presence with us; God's power and glory manifested in us and through us. He calls for us to grasp the immensity of our inheritance in Christ:

The eyes of your understanding being enlightened,
that ye may know what is the hope of His calling,
and what the riches of the glory of His inheritance in the saints.
And what is the exceeding greatness of His power to us who believe

GLORY FOREVER!

We have seen that God who commanded the light to shine out of darkness has shined His eternal glory in our hearts by our relationship with Jesus Christ (2 Corinthians 4:6-7). Out of the darkness and chaos that resulted from the fall of man comes the glorious light of God's own presence and power, in us, and through us, as we make our way through this present evil world.

Then, when we come to the end of our journey here, we enter a heavenly glory that is forever.

Our heavenly Jerusalem has no need of the sun or the moon to shine on it because the glory of God lights it up, and its lamp is the Lamb (Revelation 21:23).

The throne of God and of the Lamb shall be in it,
and His servants shall serve Him:
And they shall see His face,
and His name shall be in their foreheads
And there shall be no night there,
and they need no candle, neither light of the sun,
for the Lord God giveth them light:
and they shall reign forever and ever.
(Revelation 22:3-5)

THEREFORE, WALK AS CHILDREN OF LIGHT

God's glorious light is our inheritance and our destiny. Jesus urged His followers to believe in the light and walk as children of light (John 12:36). The Apostle Paul repeated the admonition to both the Ephesians and the Thessalonians:

Ye were sometimes darkness, but now are ye light in the Lord;
Walk as children of light (Ephesians 5:8)
Ye are all the children of light, and the children of the day:
We are not of the night, nor of darkness (1 Thess. 5:5)

It is a great tragedy if the glory in us fades, becoming almost indistinguishable from the darkness. Yet many of God's people and their churches seem to fade away from the initial brightness of that divine spark that shone in them at their new birth. They become dull, muted, lackluster – barely conscious of what is happening to them. Beware the example of Eli, the backslidden priest in the house of the Lord, who fell backwards and died, and his evil sons died, and the mother of his grandson died as she was giving birth.

And she named the child Ichabod, saying:
The glory is departed from Israel (I Samuel 4:21).

May we never share the fate of Samson in whose life the power and glory of God was so evident; yet he was a carnal man, not careful about the things of God. He woke up one day not knowing that the presence of God had left him and soon found himself blind and chained to a mill, going in circles, getting nowhere. May our churches never be likened to the church at Laodicea, seemingly rich and increased with goods and in need of nothing, yet Jesus had been driven out and stands knocking at the door, asking to be let back in (Revelation 3:14-20).

There is no sorrow so deep as that of Peter, who wept bitterly after his betrayal of Jesus. There is no blindness so intense as that of Samson. There is no church so empty as one without the presence of Jesus! Let the beauty of Jesus ever be seen in us! We are the Temple of the Living God! We are the children of Light. So let us walk, even as He walked (I John 2:6).

The world needs light! The world needs life! If it doesn't flow from us, the world has no light, no life, and no hope. The glory of God reflected in us is not natural. It does not come from us, nor from anything in this present evil world. God's glory cannot be made; it cannot be purchased; it must be given by God. If it fades in us because of unrepented sin, it must be renewed by God as we turn back to Him. To avoid darkness, we must ever walk with the Lord, hungrily seeking:

The God of peace, that brought again from the dead
our Lord Jesus,
that great shepherd of the sheep,
through the blood of the everlasting covenant,
make you perfect in every good work to do His will,
working in you that which is well-pleasing in His sight,
through Jesus Christ, to whom be glory forever and ever.
(Heb. 13:20-21)

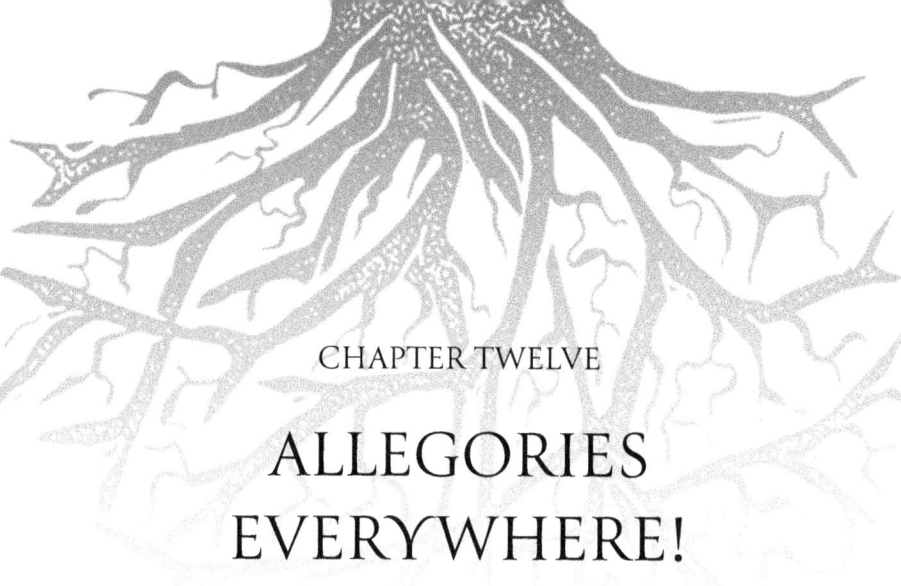

CHAPTER TWELVE

ALLEGORIES EVERYWHERE!

THIS SERIES OF MESSAGES HAS highlighted numerous Scriptural allegories. We began by looking at leprosy as a representation of the sin that lurks in each of us; then we looked at Jacob, a notable sinner, and traced his progress through life until he became a Prince of God. Jacob's story is our story!

A study of Amalek followed, picturing sin as a determined enemy that will eventually destroy us if we don't defeat it with God's help. The helmet of salvation came next, indicating that the battleground is in our minds as we wage war against sin rampant in the world, in our own fleshly nature, and against the devil, the "parent" of sin. We are then encouraged to remember who we are and where we began our spiritual journey by marking our progress towards spiritual maturity with monuments and memorials. The following message identified spiritual maturity as "keeping the Sabbath" by finding rest in our relationship with God.

We also discussed four trees that appear in Scripture – the Tree of Life and the Tree of Knowledge of Good and Evil, planted by God in Eden; the Tree of Death epitomized by the Cross, that cruel instrument of torture planted by man; and the Tree of Resurrection Life planted in heaven by our Savior. Two Brides were next in view: the still sinful earthly Bride of Christ and the glorious Heavenly Bride of Christ. Then we tracked the contrast between marital chaos (that is, our "marriage" to sin) and wedded bliss (our "marriage" to Christ). We must divorce the first before we can fully enjoy the second – anything less than complete separation from sin is likened in Scripture to adultery.

The tenth message in our series highlighted some of the many rich soulwinning allegories in Scripture, focusing on different aspects of personal evangelism. In the previous chapter we talked about God's glorious Light and the wonder of its radiance in us and through us when we become part of God's family. In this final chapter we are going to look at allegories everywhere throughout Scripture that teach about spiritual under-achievers and overcomers. Their stories raise some important questions:

- Why do some Christians succeed where others fail?
- Why do some enjoy their faith while others seem perpetually miserable?
- Why do some defeat sin and others wallow in it?

- In short, why are some Christians overcomers while others are underachievers?

ESAU

We begin with Esau, who from birth had everything in his favor. He was the eldest son, a rugged outdoor kind of man's man who was the favorite of his father. He was destined to inherit all of God's blessings from his father so that he would be the one – along with Abraham and Isaac – through whom all the world would one day be blessed. But Esau lost it all. He threw away the power of his position because he was careless. He did not appreciate his spiritual legacy but chose instead to satisfy his old nature.

- Esau was a careless man who never learned self-discipline. His will got in the way of God's will.

SAMSON

Samson had everything. He was given superhuman strength that made him invincible. He prevailed with ease against his enemies, whether human or animal. Natural barriers could not stand against him. But Samson lost it all. He threw away his power because he chose physical pleasures over spiritual submission.

- Samson was a carnal man who never learned spiritual wisdom. His life illustrates the danger of combining an unbroken will with God's power.

KING SAUL

He had everything. He was Israel's first king. He had the God of Heaven on his side to help him build the greatest kingdom the world had ever seen. But King Saul lost everything. God tore the kingdom away from him because of his pride and disobedience.

- Saul was a conceited man who never admitted his own sinfulness and never learned obedience to God. His stubborn pride removed him from God's presence and God's blessing.

JUDAS

Judas had everything. He walked in the company of Jesus Christ for more than three years. He heard Jesus' words of life. He saw Jesus' miracles. He held a trusted position among Jesus' followers. But Judas lost it all. He betrayed Jesus because he wanted power without paying the price of self-sacrifice.

- Judas was a corrupt man who sought personal gain at no personal cost. His ambition ruined his inheritance.

DEMAS

Demas had everything. He was a fellow laborer with the great Apostle Paul during the exciting days of the early Church. He heard Paul preach and teach. He may have sat and watched as

Paul wrote letters that would later become part of Scripture. But Demas lost it all. His name means "popular" and may provide a clue to his character, because Demas sold out to the world and turned his back on God. One of the saddest statements in the Bible is found in 2 Timothy 4:10, where Paul writes: "Demas hath forsaken me, having loved this present world..."

- Demas was a compromiser. He sought popularity with the world rather than condemnation from the world. His spiritual shallowness made him a sellout to the world.

DANIEL

In sharp contrast to so many underachievers in Scripture (we could add Cain to the list, and the ten Hebrew spies who gave a bad report about the Promised Land, and a long line of corrupt high priests, among many others), Daniel's life is a glorious example of quiet determination to serve God under the worst circumstances. Although he lived most of his life as a captive in a foreign land he was uncompromising in his faith and his public testimony recorded in Scripture influenced kings and kingdoms. Chapter 6 of Daniel is a good example of the impact he made on others.

PAUL

Of the many overcomers in Scripture, the Apostle Paul is perhaps the greatest example because he did so many things right. What's more, in his unsaved condition he had much more of the world to lose than most others. At a relatively young age he had risen to the pinnacle of Jewish religious life, a student of the greatest teacher in Israel, a highly respected Pharisee, blameless in his devotion to the Law, a "Hebrew of the Hebrews," perhaps an eventual candidate for High Priest. But, by his own testimony, the things that were gainful to him in this life lost all their value after he met Jesus.

What things were gain to me, those I counted loss for Christ.
Yea, doubtless, and I count all things but loss
For the excellency of the knowledge of Christ Jesus my Lord,
For whom I have suffered the loss of all things
And do count them but dung that I may win Christ.
And be found in Him, not having mine own righteousness,
Which is of the law, but that which is through the faith of Christ,
The righteousness which is of God by faith:
That I may know Him, and the power of His resurrection,
And the fellowship of His sufferings,
being made conformable unto His death…
(13b) This one thing I do,
Forgetting those things which are behind,
And reaching forth unto those things which are before
I press towards the mark for the prize
of the high calling of God in Christ Jesus.
(Philippians 3:7-10;13-14)

As a result of his complete dedication to Christ, the Apostle Paul showed us what is possible:

- His words were filled with spiritual power (I Corinthians 2:4)

  My speech and my preaching was not with enticing words of man's wisdom, but in demonstration of the Spirit and of power.

- His life was triumphant (2 Corinthians 2:14)

  Thanks be unto God, which always causeth us to triumph in Christ.

- He was strong in Christ (2 Corinthians 12:10)

  When I am weak [in things of this world], then am I strong

- He was single-minded (Philippians 3:8)

  I have suffered the loss of all things, and do count them but dung, that I may win Christ.

- Peace filled his heart (Philippians 4:7)

  The peace of God, which passeth all understanding, Shall keep your hearts and minds through Christ Jesus.

- He was content with whatever he had (Philippians 4:11)

  I have learned, in whatsoever state I am, therewith to be content.

- He was steadfast in his faith
  I know whom I have believed,
  and am persuaded that He is able to keep
  that which I have committed unto Him (2 Timothy 1:12)

Paul (and Daniel before him) triumphed when so many others failed because:

- They were not careless about spiritual things
- They were not carnal (they did not value the physical over the spiritual)
- They were not conceited (they put God first in everything)
- They were not corrupt
- They never compromised with sin, their flesh, or the devil.
- They never quit

Paul was filled with power and joy because he lived a consecrated life. He was "sold out" to Jesus Christ, who was everything to him.

UNDERACHIEVER OR OVERCOMER?

If you have Christ as your Savior, you have everything! Whatever you may think you lack, you have above all a God who loves you and makes all His power available to you to live a joyful and victorious life. Yet despite God's amazing provision and promises many Christians miss the mark, either because they don't know what is theirs in Christ, or because they are too ignorant or too lazy to apply clear principles for spiritual growth as outlined in Scripture. See 2 Peter 1:1-11.

Some are miserable because they choose to slop around in the hog-pen with the rest of the world. They and the God-deniers they associate with don't fear God. Instead, they exploit His patient mercy and grace, not seeing themselves for the spiritual losers they are, facing eternal destruction as their reward.

It's a strange quirk of human nature that habitual under-achievers will often mock and reject winners. But at some point those who mock you and scorn God may be turned to God by what they see in you. Consider the impact on others of Daniel trusting God in the lion's den, and Paul, singing hymns of praise to God at midnight, after being brutally and unfairly beaten and thrown into prison. Both men changed the lives of others and altered the course of history because God was seen in them. The Philippian jailer fell at Paul's feet and asked how to be saved. Daniel's king issued a decree that everybody in his kingdom should reverence the God of Daniel.

Considering their inspiring testimonies, the abiding question for each of us must be: Do others who know you want to worship *your* God?

ABOUT THE AUTHOR

EDWARD THAL LIVED in South Africa and England before settling in America, where he is a naturalized citizen. He serves in a ministry support role at Bluegrass Baptist Church in Georgetown, KY, has served churches in South Carolina and Virginia, and as assistant to missionary church planters in London, England, and the Channel Island of Guernsey.